Animal Body Parts

Minibeast
Body Parts

Clare Lewis

raintree

a Capstone company — publishers for children

Raintree is an imprint of Capstone Global Library Limited, a company incorporated in England and Wales having its registered office at 7 Pilgrim Street, London, EC4V 6LB – Registered company number: 6695582

www.raintree.co.uk
myorders@raintree.co.uk

Edited by Helen Cox Cannons and Shelly Lyons
Designed by Steve Mead
Picture research by Svetlana Zhurkin
Production by Victoria Fitzgerald
Originated by Capstone Global Library Ltd
Printed and bound in China

ISBN 978 1 406 29803 1
19 18 17 16 15
10 9 8 7 6 5 4 3 2 1

British Library Cataloguing in Publication Data
A full catalogue record for this book is available from the British Library.

Acknowledgements
We would like to thank the following for permission to reproduce photographs: Dreamstime: Musat Christian, cover (bottom); Getty Images: James H. Robinson, 21; Shutterstock: akkaradech, 22 (top), 23, alexsvirid, 5, bofotolux, 18, Cathy Keifer, 11, 23, Cosmin Manci, 22 (bottom), Emily Goodwin, 7, Fabio Sacchi, 9, GOLFX, 16, Ian Grainger, 14, JoeFotoSS, cover (top right), Katarina Christenson, 20, 23, mj007, back cover (right), 22 (middle), Patricia Chumillas, back cover (left), 15, pinkomelet, 23 (flower), Sam DCruz, 19, Sebastian Janicki, 8, 10, 23, Steven Russell Smith Photos, cover (top left), Valeriy Vladimirovich Kirsanov, 12, Vasiliy Koval, 13, Viktor Petruk, 4, Vitalii Hulai, 17, 23, Wojciech Koszyk, cover (top middle); Wikimedia: University of Arizona/Paul Marek, 6.

We would like to thank Michael Bright for his invaluable help in the preparation of this book.

Every effort has been made to contact copyright holders of material reproduced in this book. Any omissions will be rectified in subsequent printings if notice is given to the publisher.

All the internet addresses (URLs) given in this book were valid at the time of going to press. However, due to the dynamic nature of the internet, some addresses may have changed, or sites may have changed or ceased to exist since publication. While the author and publisher regret any inconvenience this may cause readers, no responsibility for any such changes can be accepted by either the author or the publisher.

Contents

Some words are shown in bold, **like this**. You can find out what they mean by looking in the glossary.

What is a minibeast?

Minibeasts are small animals. Minibeasts are invertebrates. This means they do not have a backbone.

Beetles, worms and spiders are minibeasts.

Minibeasts do not all look the same. Minibeasts' bodies can be very different from each other.

Let's take a look at parts of their bodies.

Legs

Spiders have eight legs. Insects have six legs.

Centipedes and millipedes have lots of legs. This millipede has up to 750 legs!

foot

mucous trail

Some minibeasts do not have legs.

Snails have one big foot. They use slime, called mucous, to help them glide along.

Wings

wing cases

wings

Most insects have wings and can fly.

Ladybirds and other beetles have wing cases. The wing cases protect their delicate wings.

Dragonflies have four wings. They can move each wing in different directions.

Dragonflies can fly fast and can even fly backwards!

Eyes

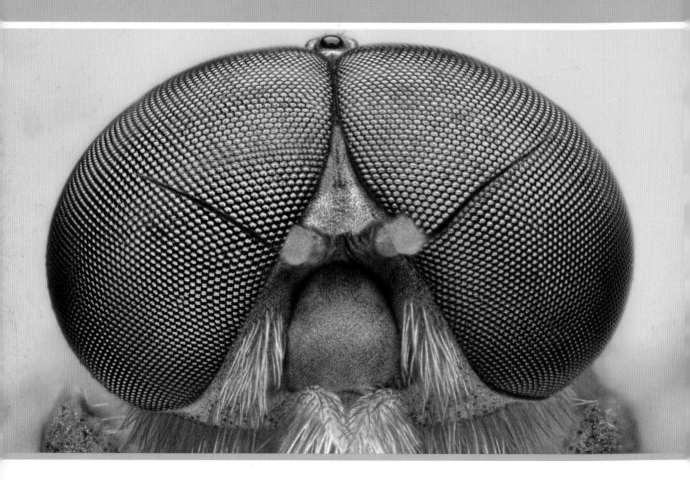

Insects have special eyes called compound eyes. Compound eyes are lots of tiny **lenses** all together.

A fly has two compound eyes. Each compound eye has around 4,000 lenses.

Most spiders have eight eyes. Most spiders can only see in black and white.

Two of this wolf spider's eyes are very large. It has good eyesight for hunting **prey**.

Antennae and tentacles

Insects have two **antennae**, or feelers, on their heads. They are covered in tiny hairs.

The hairs on their antennae help the insect to feel, smell or taste.

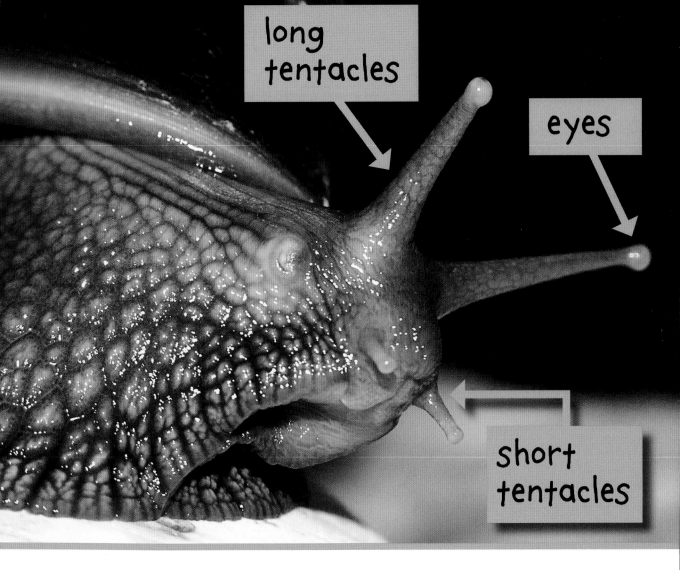

long
tentacles

eyes

short
tentacles

Snails and slugs have tentacles on their heads. A tentacle is a long, thin part of the body on an animal's mouth or head.

Tentacles are used for feeling and smelling.

Mouths

proboscis

Butterflies have a long tongue-like mouthpart. It is called a proboscis.

Butterflies use a proboscis to suck up **nectar** from flowers.

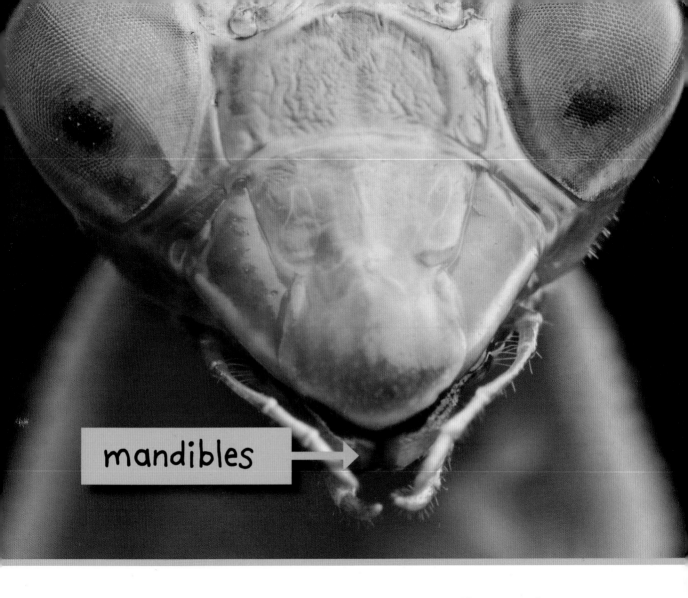

mandibles

Many insects have strong mouth parts called mandibles. They are like jawbones.

This praying mantis has strong mandibles for eating its **prey**.

Minibeast babies

Many minibeast babies look very different from their parents.

Caterpillars change to become butterflies.

Some insect babies live in water. They breathe through **gills**, like fish.

When this dragonfly nymph becomes an adult, it will leave the water and grow wings.

Body parts for protection

Snails have shells. Snails can hide inside their shells to protect their soft bodies. This keeps them safe from **predators**.

leaf insect

Some minibeast bodies and wings look like parts of plants, such as leaves. This helps a minibeast to hide from predators.

Leaf insects look just like green leaves.

Body parts for attack

Spiders trap **prey** with pointed fangs.

Liquid poison, called **venom**, runs through the fangs into prey as they bite.

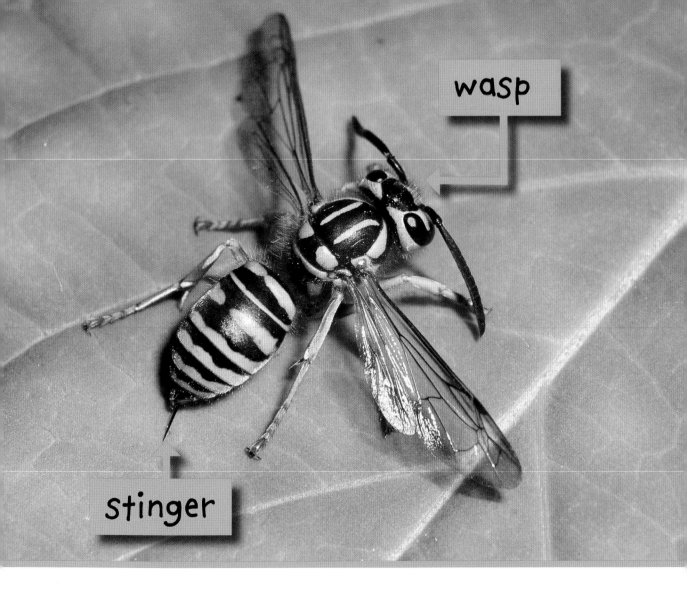

Some insects have stingers.

Bees and wasps sting if they are attacked. Venom runs through the stinger into the attacker's body.

Totally amazing minibeast body parts!

Rhinoceros beetles have long, hard horns on their heads. They use them for fighting. They also use their horns to dig into leaves and hide.

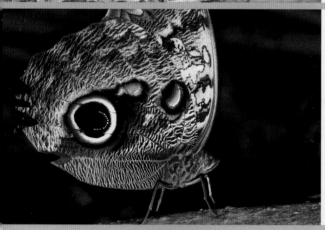

The owl butterfly has large circles on its wings. The circles look like owl eyes. This helps to scare away **predators**.

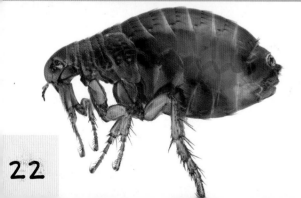

Fleas have very powerful, long legs. They use their back legs to jump 100 times their own height!

Glossary

 **gills** parts of an animal that help it to breathe under water

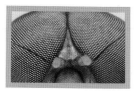 **lenses** parts of the eye that deal with light to help us see

 **nectar** sweet liquid a plant makes to attract insects

 **predator** animal that hunts other animals for food

 **prey** animal that is hunted by another animal

 **venom** liquid poison produced by some animals. Venom is put into other animals through a bite or sting.

Find out more

Books

Invertebrates (Animal Classifications), Angela Royston
(Raintree, 2015)

Life Story of a Ladybird (Animal Life Stories), Charlotte
Guillain (Raintree, 2014)

Websites

Learn about more amazing minibeasts at:
www.insects.org

Find wonderful photographs and watch videos all about
minibeasts at:
www.bbc.co.uk/nature/life/Insect

Index